CONFIDENCE WITHOUT REGRET

CONFIDENCE WITHOUT REGRET

THE BUTTERFLY EXPERIENCE

OVERCOMING LOW-SELF ESTEEM TO LIVING IN YOUR PURPOSE

SHURVONE P. WRIGHT

Book Cover Design, Interior Book Design, and Formatting- Tyora Moody: https://tywebbincreations.com

Developmental Editing- CaTyra Polland: https://www.love4words.com

Copy Editing (Proofreading)- Erica James:
https://www.masterpieceswriting.com

Cover Photography- DeAnna Lupe:
https://www.dlightfulcreations.com

Make-up- Irene Robinson: https://www.instagram.com/
Irodoes.makeuppp

TABLE OF CONTENTS

DEDICATION

This book is dedicated to my amazing husband, Roger Wright, who has watched me grow, change and transform into the woman I am today. Thank you for walking through this journey with me, for supporting me, and for loving me. I could not have done it without you.

To my daughters, Danielle, Destiny, and Rebekah Wright, you are the reason I worked so hard to overcome and to become a better version of myself. This book also is dedicated to every woman who strives to be the best version of herself and desires to walk in boldness to live the life she deserves.

To my mother and my father, Loma Porter and Walter Mitchell (may he rest in peace), who gave me all they could. Thank you for all of your life experiences and love. I love you with all my heart. In memory of my dad, who called me his warrior: Dad, I did it. I have survived it all, and I am still standing.

To Sharon Allen, aka Grammie, thank you for your love and support. Thank you for answering your phone every time I called and needed to vent. Thank you for always guiding me to God for answers.

To my grandmother, Loma Farr (may she rest in peace), who cared for me from the beginning, guided me, loved me, and showed me what it means to love unconditionally. Thank you for being a nurse for twenty-five years and for guiding me to a thirty-five-year nursing career because I watched you and learned from you. It was your example that helped me choose a career I love. Thank you for always being on your knees praying for me. I am who I am because of you, a lover of God with a love for helping people. I love you.

FOREWORD

DR. MISSY JOHNSON

Shurvone, for a long-time, lived-in fear, feeling insecure with low self-esteem and no confidence. Yet, she had an inner knowing that her life was meant to be different and impactful for others. You might be surprised how many women live their lives bound by negative voices in their heads telling them they will never change. Or they live most of their lives fighting to change the trajectory, which can be quite exhausting but rewarding—in addition to handling whatever life throws their way, including managing family, entrepreneurship, etc.

Learning to rise above life circumstances can be complicated and scary. However, when you set your mind in motion to do whatever it takes to change, amazing things happen, doors open, your mind opens, and God will open doors that seem impossible. I invite you to read this fascinating page-turner filled with wisdom and hope that will forever change and encourage you. When Shurvone asked me to write this forward, I did not hesitate because her transformation is authentic. She will help many women on their journey.

A few facts about Coach Dr. Missy Johnson: she is a survivor of a sixty-mile-per-hour car accident, a forty-seven-day coma, and stage three breast cancer. Dr. Missy is the CEO of Fearless Women Rock, LLC, a platform created for women to share their courageous stories to leverage themselves to become speakers, coaches, and authors. Dr. Missy is a BETHER screenwriter for the movie The Party. She was a keynote for the Ebony Jet Magazine platform and a speaker at the Michigan Supplier

Diversity Conference. She is a 2021 Black Enterprise Top 50 Business Coach and a Women of Excellence honoree presented by the Michigan Chronicle.

She is a recipient of President Barack Obama's Lifetime Achievement Award. Additionally, she has been featured on various media, radio, and television outlets.

Dr. Missy is an award-winning, international, three-time number-one bestselling author. She is a coach and story strategist with mastery in helping women reinvent their lives after they have reached a peak in their careers. She provides executive coaching and personal leadership development training. Dr. Missy's motto is: "Be your authentic self and create your yellow brick road so unforgettable they can't forget you."

Dr. Missy is available for speaking in the corporate arena and at church events and offers one-on-one and group coaching programs for women.

Contact Dr. Missy:
Website: iamdrmissy.com
Instagram: @AskDrmissy
Facebook: @AskDrMissy

INTRODUCTION

Have you struggled with low self-esteem and low confidence? Are you ready to live the life you deserve? Are you feeling stuck? Ready to make the transformation into the life you want and leave behind everything that does not serve you?

This book will change your life. It is a page-turner that highlights my life, my healing, and my newfound confidence. I share how this newfound confidence propelled me into a brave, new world where I am confident enough to share all aspects of myself with you in hopes that this can be an inspiration. I share my story, my life, and the tools that helped transform my life. You will be able to implement the tools provided in this book to help you transform your life. You will learn why it is important to be confident in the things you can do to not live in regret and how to walk in your purpose without fear and finally learn to be confident.

As you read about my deeply ingrained fear and

insecurities, you will see that these are no longer problems for me. I have found a solution: overcoming them by acting! Whether you are struggling with low self-esteem after past trauma, feeling trapped inside your head due to addiction, or craving fulfilling relationships again after a divorce, this book offers practical steps to help you heal.

I will take you on a journey that pushed me into entrepreneurial life. It is hard and emotional writing about these issues, but it is worth every moment of pain. I hope that through reading my story others can find their inner strength to overcome major challenges in their lives as well.

This book is a journey of my darkest depths of self-development. Low self-esteem and fears plagued my life for years because of many contributing factors that fostered my negative thoughts. The first time I remember being very afraid, I was left home alone at five years old; I am not sure why. I can remember this incident like it was yesterday.

I remember being left standing near the front door, and I just stood there and cried, waiting for someone to show up.

I remember it being dark, scary and lonely because the

location seemed so big and it felt overwhelming. It makes me sad to think about the moment that changed my life forever. That incident sat dormant in my mind and was ingrained in my soul; however, I did not realize it until I began my healing process. I came to know why being alone was so scary. I would have to deal with my own thoughts and feelings, and I was not ready for that.

It was a trait I hated about myself. It made me feel needy and insecure. It was even more frustrating because I was aware of my challenges but felt as if I could not do anything to change them. I just did not know what to do.

Another incident that contributed to my neediness and insecurities was my grandfather dying when I was nine years old. This event changed me forever. He was my father figure; he was the man who nurtured me, loved me, and made me feel secure in life. When he died, I knew my life would be different. I felt unprotected from the world. It is weird that I can remember those thoughts and feelings. It is incredibly sad because I not only predicted my future but also manifested it in some way. I manifested a life of feeling unsafe and of mistrusting men.

My insecurities were fueled by the absence of my parents also. They did not emerge in my life until I was about ten years old, from what I can remember. My grandmother raised me alone after my grandfather died until I was eighteen years old, which was an extremely complicated dynamic. Being raised by my grandmother, I always felt alone. I felt as though I should never complain, so I accepted life as it was. It is not that she did not love me or make me feel unloved. There were times I feared for my life when living with my grandmother and times when things were good and I loved life. It was confusing at times because we never talked about the times when life was hard or when scary things happened. I learned early that I would have to figure things out in life, and I somehow knew I would be okay. I knew I would make it. I now know the Holy Spirit was looking out for me and guiding me.

God always meets you where you are. I had a deep knowing at an early age that I would have a better life no matter what. Not being with my parents created abandonment issues and insecurities because I grew up with instability. I always felt on guard. I became timid, quiet, and observant of my surroundings. I can remember people commenting "she is so shy" or "she is so quiet". I did not realize until later in life that I had developed low self-esteem and low confidence, but in my head, I defined it as needy. I was afraid of life.

When I was fourteen years old, boys came into my life,

and that is when I think the insecurities and low self-esteem really kicked in. I allowed boys to use and abuse me. I remember I lost my virginity in an apartment complex with a boy I did not like and, of course, he broke up with me shortly after. It was the most degrading experience I could have experienced as a young woman. I still can see the room with white walls and the mattress on the floor. I remember wanting to say "no, stop", but I could not find my voice. I could not get the words out. I just let it happen. I was scared and felt so alone in that moment.

I then had multiple so-called boyfriends who used me for sex, finally settling with one at fifteen years old and staying with him until I was twenty-one years old. I allowed my low self-esteem, low confidence, and insecurities to shape my decisions and to keep me from living a fulfilled life for many years until I decided I wanted to change.

However, with all the challenges I faced, I always knew my life would be better. I always had a never-give-up attitude, a let's-try-again mindset, no matter what happened. I do not know where that came from, other than God helping me and watching over me. Over the years, through mistakes, heartaches, failures, and lessons learned, I have evolved, finally accepting myself, growing, and developing my self-esteem and confidence. It was through continued work on myself, having a never-give-up attitude, forgiving myself, and learning from my mistakes that I evolved from a caterpillar to a butterfly, the true definition of the butterfly experience. This was a lifelong process, forty years to be exact. I hope this book will help shorten your journey to peace. In this book, you will learn how I overcame many obstacles, challenges, fears, and insecurities to become a confident author, business owner, coach, and speaker. I am a professional nurse of thirty-five years, a mother of three amazing daughters, all college graduates, a wife of twenty-nine years, and a grandmother of one beautiful granddaughter. I have two businesses: Everything Wright LLC and La' BossPreneur Marketing and Publishing LLC. I have co-authored five books and appeared in multiple magazines. I am also a contributing writer for two magazines. I started two Facebook groups: La' BossPreneur Marketing and Publishing LLC and Confidence Without Regret.

Recently, after dreaming of a beautiful butterfly and noticing major hair loss, I accepted my diagnosis of alopecia, shaved my hair off, embraced my beauty, and boldly walked in my power. I hope you explore how to walk unapologetically in your boldness and life's journey. I will walk you through my journey and the steps I took to overcome the challenges in my life to live my best life and to start living out my dreams. I hope you will identify what is holding you back from living your best life, bringing your gifts to the world and living unapologetically. My prayer is that you are motivated to start a business or to become an author, a coach, or whatever your heart desires. This book is a page-turner. You will not want to put it down. Get comfortable and get ready to change your life forever.

LOW SELF-ESTEEM

"Many non-assertive people and people with low self-esteem find they're missing opportunities in life; they often let opportunities escape them. I had to learn how to push past this and step outside of my comfort zone to live my best life."

-Shurvone

We all want to feel protected and loved. At the core of my being, that is what I desired as a child and still want today. When I am protected and loved, I feel on top of the world. Sometimes a specific event in life can take that feeling of protection away and change you forever. This is what happened to me. I am amazed by how I survived so many life events that stripped me of feeling protected, loved, and understood by those whom I loved. How did I have the instinct to fight for my life, a life to be better, to do better? I now know it was the Holy Spirit guiding me and protecting me, helping me to regain my self-esteem and confidence to live my best life and to live in my purpose. It was a long journey but one for which I am forever grateful. I overcame obstacles that easily could have derailed my life forever.

I am the oldest of three children. I have a younger sister and brother, who I love dearly. We all have different fathers. We grew up in different homes, with different experiences, but with a family that loved us. We love one another very much. However, our lives took quite different turns. I assume I ended up living with my grandmother because I was the first one born. My mother had me at sixteen years old, so I guess the best place for me was my grandparents. That is where my life began.

That time period is special to me because I can remember being a happy, carefree child. I remember running and playing. I remember playing outside, playing with family, playing with the kids at school, and feeling safe. The freedom of a child is wonderful. As I write this sentence, I find it crazy how I can remember what it felt like to be free and unbothered about life and to have fun with no worries.

Our family lived in a big, beautiful home in San Francisco until I was five years old. I remember the home vividly. I can visualize how big it was, all the rooms, and the backyard. My auntie, who was only a year older than me, and I often spent time with my grandfather in his garden. He had a lush garden with big leafy collard greens and other vegetables. I remember my aunt and I being able to run and to play if we wanted; my grandfather never seemed to worry about us messing anything up. He simply allowed us to be free.

My grandfather always worked in his shed. He would let us play around him. He never made me feel unwanted or as if I bothered him. One day, he was building a China cabinet. I remember thinking it was so big and pretty. I am not sure why this stuck in my memory, but over the years, I wanted one in my home. Fifty-one years later, I have his China cabinet. My grandfather made me feel safe and loved. I made this memory a part of the book because just like painful memories, happy memories can stay with you for a lifetime, and my grandfather made me happy.

Shortly after I turned five, we moved from San Francisco to Daly City, California, where my grandparents purchased their second home. I lived there off and on until I was eighteen years old. There were many happy moments and many scary moments that changed my life and molded who I am today. The happy times included spending time with my grandparents and learning how to cook in their home. I remember the first time I cut up a chicken. Sometimes I would sit in the kitchen all day during the holidays watching and learning. My grandmother taught me hygiene and how to be a young lady. It was not always perfect, but she formed me into the woman I am today. The most amazing experience and lesson my grandmother taught me was to love God and to pray. She loved God and she stayed on her knees in prayer.

Having grandparents is so special. Their influence changed the course of my life and sustained me throughout my life. I experienced the most stability in my grandparents' home. At times, it was hard and felt unstable, but out of all the places I have lived, living there felt the safest. I know my grandmother did her absolute best to bring peace to our home. She took good care of me and did the best she could. I knew she loved me.

However, I always felt as if I were a burden. I am not sure at what age I began feeling this way, but I do remember acting on those feelings when I was twelve or thirteen. I just stopped asking for things. I did not

4

want to be a bother. It probably came from the realization that my grandmother had raised five of her six kids and I was the bonus kid. I honestly cannot say where those feelings came from. As children, we hear and see things and maybe that is what happened. I must have heard or experienced something that made me feel like a burden. I still feel this way, which is why it is so hard for me to ask for help or to lean on anyone for support. Don't get me wrong. I do those things, but it does not come naturally.

Yes, I grew up in a household with domestic violence. Even though this was long ago and I have my own home now, I have nightmares about it from time to time. Trauma certainly can be lifelong. My grandparents were extremely loving, and they loved God. I am a believer in God because of them. I chose to be a nurse because of my grandmother, and I married a man like my grandfather.

Experiencing my grandfather's death at nine years old changed me forever. It was the beginning of a long journey that took me years to overcome.

One day he was reading me stories at night, playing with me, and being the best grandfather any child could have. It seemed like overnight he was sick in bed and rushed to the hospital. At the time, I did not know what was going on but later found out it was cancer. As a child, I had no concept of time, so I had no idea how long he was in the hospital. The one time I remember visiting him at the hospital, I remember what seemed like a long walk down the hospital hallway then being in his room and seeing him lying in bed. I was scared and confused. I can remember him lying in the hospital bed with other family members around him as well. I just wanted to know when he could come home. I do not recall much detail from that day, other than being there and being scared. That was the last time I saw him alive.

I was blessed to have my grandfather in my world for nine years. Those nine years have affected my entire life. The only true happiness I experienced as a child was when he was alive. His death is one of my most painful experiences. I can remember him being my protector, playing with me, reading me stories, and allowing me to be a kid. He loved me and protected me.

I still can see the work overalls he wore almost daily. They were off-white, thick, durable, and paint-stained. He was always fixing and building something.

When my grandfather was around, I felt unique, safe, and secure. He gave me so much love and fatherly affection. Thinking about it makes me smile. My grandfather would walk me to school. I would watch him work in the garden or in the shed. He never made me feel as if I was bothering him. I felt genuinely loved; he would let me play and be in his presence.

I do not have any memory of what happened between the time he died and the funeral. I only remember falling to the ground at his funeral and crying hysterically to the point I had to be carried out. I felt as if my life would forever be changed. I felt unprotected in the world. I knew my life would be different; I somehow knew it would be hard. How did I know this? How could I predict my life at nine years old?

Once my grandfather died, my grandmother retired from her nursing job and focused on raising me and my auntie. Her other children were grown and out of the house. During this time, there were good experiences, while others were scary. One of my family members was a drug user. When he was around, it was terrifying because we never knew when he would have an outburst, and we never knew when they would end.

Life became quite confusing for me because after those outbursts, or my mother and father's attempts to care for me, things would seemingly go back to what was considered normal. We did not talk about the scary incidents or how the occurrences in my life affected me.

My grandmother did her best to take care of me, but with my grandfather being gone, I felt exposed and unprotected.

2

MY INNOCENCE
WAS STOLEN

"A child's heart is pure and so ready to please the world, yet so ready to learn how to live in it. In one day, the eyes of a child are no longer pure but pain."

-Shurvone

I wonder how no one knew a family friend molested me, and for the sake of the family, I will not mention his name.

I was so young and so scared when he would put his hand up my dress, either touching or rubbing me. It felt creepy and wrong. However, all I could do was smile and stand there. I thought if I did nothing and said nothing, he would stop. However, it did not stop. It continued for way too long.

The molestation, I resolved in my mind, was not wrong because he did not penetrate me but would put his hands under my dress. I felt frozen with fear, not knowing what to do. I knew it was wrong, but I could not scream. I could not move his hand or run. I just sat there. I never told anyone or exposed the person who did this because I honestly did not think anyone would believe me. I soon learned how to overlook behaviors and to keep silent to protect people who did not deserve my loyalty.

It is disheartening to think about this incident. I developed a bad habit of overlooking people's horrible behavior and of second-guessing myself. I ignored and discounted my internal discernment. The molestation affected my entire life and interfered with my relationships. I did not trust people, but I hated being alone, so I ended up in a relationship with someone I did not trust. Because I hated being alone, I put up with anything. I put up with cheating, disappointments, lies, and so much more that did not serve me well.

When I was twelve, my mother decided she wanted my sister and brother to live with her and her then-boyfriend, a pimp, drug dealer, and an evil man. He created another level of fear and insecurity because he would beat my mother for what seemed like anything. The crazy and sick part, he was kind to me and my siblings. He would tell me how smart I was. He made me feel as if he would never harm us, but I never knew how far he would go to hurt my mother, or when another beating would happen. I soon learned how to be a people pleaser. I just wanted to make sure I kept everything around me perfect, kept everyone happy, hoping to prevent my mom from getting another beating. I tried to make sure she did not say or do anything that would provoke him. I tried to make sure everything was clean and tidy so that he would not have anything to say or possibly beat my mother. Sometimes it worked, and sometimes it did not. I walked around most of the time with a knot in my stomach, on edge, while pretending everything was okay. I put on a fake smile and watched and waited for the subsequent explosion.

I vividly can see our Christmas tree sitting by the window. There were so many presents underneath it. It was decorated nicely. It was the first Christmas I celebrated with my mother, sister, and brother. I was bouncing around the house, thinking things had changed. I thought maybe this would be the change I longed for, to have a perfect family and to feel safe. I wanted an exciting, happy feeling, where I could jump and hop around with childlike joy. I just wanted to feel normal and safe.

That all came to a screeching halt because my mother's boyfriend had an explosive outburst and when that happened, we never knew what would happen next. The pit of my stomach would hurt when this happened. I felt helpless and scared. The next thing I remember was him throwing the Christmas presents out the window and pushing her face through the window. He broke the window with her face. I felt so sick to my stomach. Fear rose in me like never before. It was one of the scariest events in my life. We later hid in the closet, hoping things would calm down. I do not remember if she went to the hospital. I remember not knowing what to do, what to say, or how to act. I was nervous, shaking, and afraid. This event altered my life. I was fearful, insecure, and a people-pleaser. When I think back on all the events that scared and traumatized me, I know now it was God who protected me and my mind. I honestly do not know how I made it without being on drugs or mentally unstable. Honestly, I am surprised to still be alive.

Soon after I landed back with my grandmother, my mother did her best to come back to take care of me, but they were failed attempts. The back and forth further solidified my fears and insecurities. I also went to live with my father for a few months when I was fifteen years old, which was short-lived when I walked in on him shooting up drugs. Sadly, I knew what he was doing. I do not know how I knew, but I knew. I was in shock and in disbelief. I felt betrayed and disappointed. I was frozen with fear and did not know what to do. All I wanted to do was get out. Again, I landed back at my grandmother's home.

My mother suffered from drug addiction and the issues that accompanied it. She tried her best to take care of us, but it never came together. Not having my mother to care for me affected me. Her absence and poor parenting increased my fear and insecurities. I just wanted a normal life with my mom and dad caring for me. My mother has been clean for over twenty-five years and my father has gone on to be with the Lord. May he rest in peace.

I attended two different junior high schools and three different high schools while my mother tried to care for me and my siblings. I do not remember much from those years. It is sad to know I did not make many friends. I did not participate in any sports or join any clubs. I do not know how I made it through, other than the Holy Spirit guiding and protecting me. I regret not having the experience of having a lot of friends, going to sports events, hanging out, and having what I call the high school experience. Again, I felt as if my childhood had been ripped away from me. I wonder at times what was so traumatic that I cannot remember what happened in middle school and high school. One thing that stands out in my memory is that I did finish early. How in the world did that happen? I attribute it to that eternal fight and determination that I was born with. How I finished with good grades and graduated early is beyond me, but thinking back, I am so proud of myself.

During this time, I also remember feeling lonely in a house full of family. I became more of an introvert, scared to speak up and to share my needs, not knowing how my life would change yet again. When your innocence is taken, it changes the core of your being. Sometimes the taint is irreversible. It took many years for me to recover from this period of my life. I know that I failed many times even though I wanted to heal. I kept praying and trying. I never gave up. Where did the fight in me come from? I honestly believe it was God.

3

THE EFFECT

"Never underestimate the effect your words and actions have on a child."

-Shurvone

My self-esteem was destroyed because of so many traumatic experiences that occurred early in my life. There are big gaps in my life before I was twenty years old that I do not remember. I often wonder why. I can remember the trauma, but there are several gaps. I believe it is because of self-preservation that my mind will not allow me to remember certain events and time periods.

I do not remember having many friends or going to hang out at friends' houses, except for one of my friends in the neighborhood. I did not talk much at family gatherings; I would sit there in silence most times. I would *cringe* if any man looked at me or wanted to hug me because I thought it would be another molestation experience, another violation of my body, and the thought of that made me sick.

However, my low self-esteem influenced me to allow boys to use my body against my will. Losing my virginity to a boy in an apartment at fourteen years old was the worst feeling ever; I felt ashamed, dirty and disgusted. To this day, I do not know why I allowed it, but I did. The shame came from knowing he did not care for me and instead wanted to use me. In my head, I said no, but I could not get the words out. My throat would not let go of the words, "no, I don't want to do this." I lay there, allowing him to have sex with me. It felt more like rape. Then there was Tommy, who I met and dated from age fourteen until I was twenty, which changed my world. I was naive and easily swayed to do things I did not want to do. Whatever he told me, I believed, and I did whatever he wanted me to do. I hung onto his every word and direction. I loved him. I needed to have someone to love and to feel loved. He made me laugh all the time. I felt needed and desired by him. I felt in my gut that he would take care of me and protect me. I clung to him no matter what happened or how he treated me.

Tommy was never physically or verbally abusive. However, there was mental abuse because I allowed him to convince me to get five abortions over a six-year period, which haunted me for years until I was able to forgive myself. This took many years of self-talk, prayer, and counseling. I was so lost and desperate to be loved by a man that I let him talk me into killing my babies. I also take responsibility for letting it happen; however, I just could not say no to Tommy. I do not know how I managed to get through that painful period. How did I handle it mentally? I cannot tell you, other than just blocking it out at the time. Later in my life, I learned how to forgive myself and know that God forgave me.

Four years into the relationship, I found out Tommy smoked marijuana. Can you imagine I dated him for four years and did not know he was smoking marijuana? I swore I would never use any type of drug.

I experienced firsthand what drugs can do and how they can destroy lives. My mother was a drug user for a long time and went to prison, among many other things. My father was addicted to heroin until he died. I never wanted to travel down that road of addiction. Soon after I discovered Tommy was using marijuana daily, I found out he was using cocaine also.

One night, Tommy introduced me to cocaine, not only cocaine but also crack. We were sitting in his car parked on a dark side street. I loved how it made me feel; it was the best feeling ever. I felt a sense of calm, peace, and relaxation I never had experienced in my life. In a matter of minutes, my life had changed. I abused drugs for two years straight. I went to work high; I went around family high. I could not believe I had become the person I said I would never become. However, I allowed my low self-esteem and my need to please Tommy take me down this road.

Those two years were the lowest I had ever felt, but I knew that one day life would be different and better. I just did not know how to make things better. The euphoric feeling I received from getting high held me hostage, until one day I was lying in bed after getting high all night. I felt so depressed and scared that I could not get out of bed.

Laying there for what seemed like an eternity, I heard a voice in my head say, "You're going to die if you don't stop." At that moment, I was set free from drugs. I never went to any counseling or support group. I called a friend who helped me get out of bed, go to her church, and rededicate my life to God. I was so scared and ashamed, but she stood with me as I gave my life back to God. When I gave up drugs, I decided to leave Tommy because he would not give up drugs. So I left him. I soon had to figure out what I wanted to do with my life. I was technically homeless and did not have anyone to live with because I was embarrassed about my life.

I ended up at the Los Angeles Job Corp, a nursing program that put me on a path to having a highly successful thirty-five-year nursing career. I needed to dig myself out of the pit of low self-esteem, not feeling as if my voice mattered. I know now God helped me in all that I experienced and helped me pursue my fantastic career. Considering all that I experienced, I always rose above the ashes.

When I arrived at the nursing program, I was broken and terrified, but I was determined to finish. I was afraid and felt alone. I also believed this was my last chance to get my life together even though I was only twenty-one. It was not my last chance, but it sure felt like it.

I remember being dropped off in front of this tall, brick building and taken to the thirteenth floor, where I would live for two years. The fear set in quickly. I could feel myself shutting down, but I had to pull it together and figure out how I would make it because I had to.

The intake counselor walked me to my room, which looked like a dorm room and made me feel lonely for some reason. Over the next few years, all I did was study and go to school, which helped me graduate at the top of my class. A few months before the graduation, I met Joe, who disguised himself as a man of God because he taught bible study and was a deacon in the church. A few months after meeting him, he talked me into marrying him.

As Joe and I stood at the courthouse alone, I felt scared with no family and no friends. When the justice of the peace instructed me to say I do and those words left my mouth, I wanted to suck them back in. An overwhelming sense of dread came over me; I knew it was wrong, and it felt wrong. I had no idea what was about to take place in my life. Now that I think back, my gift of discernment and intuition knew we were not good and the marriage was not going to be good. I felt trapped and knew things were not right. Joe soon became verbally abusive. When he raised his voice, I felt fear rise in the pit of my stomach, and I would try to do whatever it took to calm the situation.

We rely on past behavior mechanisms and coping methods when we experience similar traumatic experiences. We default to old behaviors because it is ingrained in us. We must unlearn those responses and replace them with productive and healthy options.

It did not take much to upset Joe. All I had to do was not agree with him. As time went on, he eventually would yell at me in public. I became more and more afraid after he slapped me for the first time. He believed I talked back and commented too many times on something he said. I began thinking about how I let this happen to me. How could I get myself in a relationship like this?

Of course, things got worse. Joe lost his job, and I was the only one with an income. Once that happened, his anger increased and his patience disappeared. I became more afraid of him. During a discussion, I made a smart remark because I was fed up and decided I would be bold and talk back. He walked into the bathroom and knocked me on the floor. I passed out for a moment and woke up on the floor. I was so scared, and at that moment, I felt like I was repeating the life my mother lived when I was a child. A few days later, I decided to leave because if he did that to me again, I would kill him. Oh, that sounds horrible, but those were my thoughts. I did not want to relive my childhood. So instead of the latter, I decided to come up with a plan to leave. Every day, I would pack a box and tuck it in the closet. I was scared he would discover the boxes, but he never did. I just continued my plan to leave when he went to work one day.

When I was ready to leave, I waited for him to leave for work. I was so scared and anxious. I felt like a failure, but I knew I had to go. I had one paycheck, essential papers, and my clothes. I left everything else behind to start over. As I packed the car, I was extremely anxious, thinking he would come back home and catch me. I was embarrassed because the apartment complex residents watched me load the car. Once it was packed, we drove 400 miles back to my haven, my grandmother's home. Yet again, I was starting over. I felt lost, but deep down, I knew I had to figure life out. I began nursing school because I was running from a man and a life I did not want; I finished nursing school running from a man and a life I did not want. I was exhausted. I had to start my life over again.

WHY DOES THIS KEEP HAPPENING?

"No matter how hard things get in life, rememberGod is always with you."

-Shurvone

As I began rebuilding my life, I met my current husband, Roger. We have been married for twenty-eight years. When we first met, I immediately liked him; he seemed to be a genuine, kind-hearted person. However, I was transitioning from my former verbally abusive husband, and we just became friends. He was someone I could easily talk to, so we talked often about what I was going through.

I was so broken at twenty-five years old. I felt scared

and confused. When I left Joe, I had only one paycheck, my clothes, and my important papers, and I still was willing to give him half of my salary, which was only about $950.00. I do not know why I felt guilty for leaving and why I thought I had to help take care of an abusive grown man. I am not sure if it was because he stripped me of what remained of my self-esteem. I do not know what I was thinking. Why did I feel sorry for my abuser? As I think back, he was manipulative, disguising himself to be a good person and using his involvement in the church to make me believe he was a kind-hearted person. The one thing I am so grateful for is, we never had children together. It took two years to complete the divorce because he kept delaying it, hoping I would come back.

During the two-year period, I met Roger, my current husband. When we met, I immediately knew he was a kind person, and someone I wanted to get to know and have in my life.

Roger and I became closer friends during the two-year process of my divorce from Joe but did not date. I still had not healed from my past relationships. Therefore, I repeated the same behaviors, allowing other men to use me. I had sex when I did not want to, which always left me feeling empty and lonely.

I hated feeling that way and wanted to have someone in my life. I was mentally unhealthy but decided to see how Tommy was doing and if he had changed his life. I soon found out he was the same; not much had changed. He was the same old charismatic charmer who would try to convince me to do what he wanted and needed. I fell for it a few times, but something in my soul gave me the courage to say no. I think I was beginning to reach a place of being tired of being used, but it was not enough because then I met Tony, who I quickly fell in love with but did not think ever loved me. I am not sure why we even dated for the brief time we did. The breakup was awful and extremely painful, so painful that it finally broke me. I had enough of the heartbreaks; I had enough of men using me. I wanted to change my life and to heal my soul desperately. I had no idea how to do that; I had no idea how I *would* change. I was tired of it happening to me.

When I decided to change and heal, the divorce was final. I was not dating. I was broken and confused. I was tired of being tired and broken. I believe I had finally hit rock bottom in relationships. I kept wondering why this keeps happening to me? Why can't I stand up for myself? Why can't I be strong and bold and speak my mind?

I was ready to begin healing myself. When I decided to stop trying to do life without God and allowed him to become the leader of my life, that is when things began to change. For the first time in my life, I felt as if things would get better, and they did for several years.

Roger and I began dating and got married two years later. When we kissed for the first time, I knew he would be my husband. However, our marriage almost did not happen. I had abused my body, had multiple abortions, and stopped taking birth control. I also stopped having a regular period, so I thought I could not have children. One day, Roger and I found out I was pregnant. I was confused, scared and shocked. Roger and I did not live together. We were just dating, so again, I allowed a man to convince me to abort our baby. I think that baby was a boy, and I was so regretful and sad whenever I would think about him and the other children I aborted. At the time, I felt a sense of deep sadness. I have worked through this pain, asked God to forgive me, and forgiven myself, but it was a hard life lesson. I do not wish it on anyone.

Roger and I worked through that ordeal, and early in 1993, I became pregnant again. I decided this time, no matter what, I was not going to abort this child. Roger and I decided to get married before the baby was born, so we planned a wedding on a $5,000 budget. We had an intimate and beautiful wedding. We chose everything, flowers, food, a photographer, all of it. It was unique and beautiful. It was held at my auntie and uncle's home in their backyard with about seventy-five family and friends. I was on top of the world. I was six months pregnant at the ceremony and feeling very fat, but happy. I married the love of my life and life was good. We honeymooned in Hawaii, my first ever trip outside of California. It was so exciting to finally believe I was living a perfect life. I had found the man of my dreams; I was having a baby. I had traveled further than I had ever flown. I felt on top of the world.

Roger and I moved into our first two-bedroom apartment to prepare for the baby. At this point, I started a job in the outpatient drug and rehab center at the veteran's hospital in Palo Alto, California. Things were going well as we planned for the baby. We were happy being a new family and enjoying one another.

As my pregnancy progressed, I began not feeling well at seven and a half weeks. One night at work, for some reason, I kept monitoring my blood pressure. Once my shift ended, it had increased to about 140/90, which was high for me as my usual was 110/60. I drove an hour home after the shift. Once I got home, I called

Roger and told him I was not feeling well and believed I needed to go to the doctor. He said, "Okay, I will take you in the morning." I lay there, thinking about how I felt and how scared I was being alone. I believe the Holy Spirit told me not to wait until morning. He instructed me to drive myself to the doctor. I did just that, and I did not leave the hospital until twelve days later.

I received a diagnosis of pre-eclampsia, which turned into HELLP syndrome, a severe and life-threatening condition. The only way to stop it was to deliver the baby by c-section. However, my platelet count was too low for the procedure, and they wanted to keep the baby inside me for one more week. Therefore, for one week, I suffered and thought I would die. The doctors even told Roger to begin preparing for my death because the baby and I might not survive.

By the grace of God and the fantastic doctors and nurses, we both survived. Danielle weighed only 3 pounds, 8 ounces. She had to stay in the NICU for a month. The traumatic part was having an emergency c-section and then not being able to see Danielle for two days. I cried and felt so depressed because all I wanted was my baby, but I could not have her. Those two days seemed like forever. As my healing began and Danielle stabilized, they allowed me to visit her in the NICU. It was the most memorable and best feeling in the world to hold my baby for the first time. It is something I will never forget.

Roger and I shared those first few moments holding her and basking in the moment we finally became parents. It was one of the happiest days of our lives. I can remember holding her, looking at this little human that I now called my daughter. She was so little and pink.

Danielle was my little princess. I remember sitting in the wheelchair in my hospital gown as she was wrapped in her baby blanket. Roger was right by my side beaming with joy. I also could tell he was nervous but happy Danielle and I survived. After I left the hospital, Danielle remained in the NICU for another thirty days until she gained a few pounds. Roger and I visited her every day. We learned how to begin life with a newborn. The staff taught us how to bathe, clothe, and feed her. She was so little; it was scary and exciting at the same time.

Finally, it was the big day; we could bring Danielle home. We had been waiting for this special day for what seemed like forever. We bought a special outfit and her cute little car seat to the hospital. I remember what I wore on that special day, black leggings and a black blouse, proudly walking into the hospital to pick up our baby girl. We packed her up, took pictures with all the nursing staff and doctors who cared for her, then we took her home.

As we arrived home, we parked in front of our apartment building and prepared to exit the car. I noticed a brown envelope on the floor. As I proceeded to pick it up and open it, there it was—betrayal in my face. My world turned upside down in a matter of minutes. It went from the happiest day of my life to the worst day of my life. I went from thinking I knew my husband to not knowing him at all. I was heartbroken. I was emotionally drained and scared. The man who I thought would never break my heart had broken my heart.

Over the next few months, we did not speak much about the incident but decided to focus on raising our daughter, Danielle. However, when she was about a year old, I decided to leave Roger because our situation worsened. We stopped communicating, our intimacy was non-existent, and I did not know what to do. I was devastated and confused. I thought the man of my dreams would never disappoint me, but life has a way of showing you that you should never put anyone on a pedestal. Only God should hold the number one spot, but I did not know that for a long time.

It was an extremely hard year. I moved out and we managed to work things out, good enough to move back in with one another. However, we had several issues to resolve. We needed to work on building our trust and communication. I needed to work on my anger.

It was a long, hard road for us to get to a good place, but before we could, I allowed another man into my heart. He saw an opportunity to jump into my life knowing I was in a vulnerable state, and I took the bait and eventually had an affair with this person. The day I gave in to him, I was so confused, knowing in my heart that it was wrong, but at the time I needed someone to understand me. I thought this would fix everything, but it felt so wrong when I wanted it to feel right. I eventually broke it off and confessed to Roger about the whole thing and, of course, it broke him, and we had more to overcome. We began counseling and decided to give our lives back to God, started going to church, and turned our lives around. Our communication was the most challenging part of the healing process. We struggled for a long time until one day Roger said he forgave me for my infidelity and I forgave him for his infidelity, hurting me and betraying my trust.

Roger and I had to start over. As we began our healing journey, low self-esteem and self-doubt kicked in again. However, the fight I had in me kept me going and doing whatever I could do to stay positive, to stay focused, and to stay motivated to get through those challenging times.

We worked hard to heal and to reach a better place. It was not easy. However, we knew we wanted to be together, and we wanted to raise our family together. We loved one another. The biggest lesson I learned was forgiving myself. Knowing that God had forgiven me was the first step to healing. I desperately wanted to heal.

5

GETTING IT TOGETHER FOR MY DAUGHTERS

"When you become a parent, your children become your why, the reason you strive to be the best version of yourself."

-Shurvone

As I began my journey to healing, well at least partial healing, I reflected on my grandmother and my mother, who both gave me the strength I did not know I had. My grandmother loved others right where they were, always prayed, and was an example of someone who persevered through challenging times. My mother fought her way through addiction, prison, and being connected to a drug dealer and an abusive life. As I think back, I am amazed by how they both survived and managed to create a life worth living.

I watched my grandmother retire at fifty-five years old and run a household until she passed at ninety-three. She lived on what she earned and on what she accomplished. I watched her pray for everyone, love everyone, and support everyone. I realized during my healing process that my grandmother's influence on my life was strong. My lifelong goal is to stay motivated to improve my journey in life.

My journey of healing began with me going back to church and rededicating my life to God. I also had to learn how to forgive my mother for the life we did not have. I was so angry with her for not raising me, for not being the mother I wanted her to be. I was in my mid-thirties when I realized I needed to forgive my mother.

One day, Roger and I were in our first home, and he asked me why I always snapped at my mother. I was shocked that he noticed because I did not realize I was doing it. When you don't forgive, anger has a way of showing up in your life when you least expect it. I learned that forgiving is crucial, so you have room to grow and heal. Forgiving someone is not for them but the one forgiving. As I think back, I found every opportunity to let her know I was still angry. Regardless of what she did, it was not enough. I was angry she did not raise me. I was angry that she went to prison. I was angry she chose men over me. I was angry because she could not get it together. It was painful not having the mother you dream of, the mother you expect to have in life.

Once I became a mother, my relationship with my mother was more painful. I would feel sad thinking about all the mother/daughter moments that did not happen. But I knew I had to get past my past pain to be the best mother possible. During this part of my life, Roger and I had one child, Danielle. We decided we did not want any more kids because of how difficult the pregnancy was. When she turned three, we considered adoption; we wanted a boy at this time. We began praying for a boy. We would say our prayers and include our little girl in the prayers, and one day, Danielle said: "Thank you, Jesus, for my little sister." God heard her prayers, and He opened a door for us to adopt a little girl.

Adopting Destiny was a God thing. I knew of Destiny through her grandmother Sharon before she became our daughter. Sharon and I worked together at the veteran's hospital for several years, soon becoming good friends and later my confidant and mentor. We would spend time talking about life and things I needed help with on the job. It was certainly a divine meeting and connection. We worked together for a few years, and by then, we both had gotten married and Roger and I had Danielle. Over the years, Sharon would talk about Destiny, who was her husband's daughter's child. When Destiny turned three, things became too difficult for Sharon to care for her because of her marital issues. She had to make an awfully hard decision to consider placing her up for adoption. Once she prayed through her decision, God began working out His plan. I honestly believe once you allow God to take control, He will work his plan perfectly and purposefully.

One day, Sharon was on her way to the human resources office to remove Destiny from her insurance because she could not take care of her anymore. She was considering placing Destiny up for adoption, and at that moment, I said, "We will take her." As soon as I said it, I could not believe what had come out of my mouth, but it felt right. I went home and told Roger what had happened. We prayed about it, then we told Sharon and her husband Andrew we wanted to adopt Destiny.

So, the process began. In a few short months, I became

the mother of two beautiful daughters. Destiny was three and a half years old when we began the process. We first had to become her foster parents. Wow, that was a scary process because we had to get fingerprinted, sign all types of government papers, and receive an assigned social worker who visited our home once a week. Eventually, the visits lessened. However, when the social worker did visit, we had to show her a binder of things we were required to keep track of to ensure we were following all the rules and policies.

We were doing our best to be perfect and to follow all the rules. Soon after Destiny moved in, she got pneumonia. Shortly thereafter, she fell off the bunk bed and we had to take her to the emergency room. I thought for sure they would take her away from us. Oh my God, we were so scared.

We managed to get through an incredibly challenging beginning, going from a family of three to a family of four and managing Destiny's separation anxiety from her grandparents. However, a few months into the process, the courts informed us we might lose her because her mother and possibly the maternal grandmother wanted custody. It was heart-wrenching to think we could lose her. In the end, we did not lose her and six months later, we finalized her adoption and she became our legal child, Destiny Wright. We were excited and nervous about how all of this would work because it was an open adoption. We wanted her to see her other family eventually and to meet her mother one day. We also wanted Sharon and Andrew to be in our lives because they had raised Destiny until she became our child. So again, we had to adjust our lives and implement a whole new process of how we functioned as a family. Sharon and Andrew affectionately became Grammy Sharon and Grandpa AJ.

The transition into becoming a mother of two was harder than I expected because we had to adjust to include the biological grandparents and to figure out how that would work. We had to help Danielle adjust to having a new sister because she was four and had been an only child. She was spoiled and loved not only by her parents but also by all. She received extra love because of the traumatic entrance she made into the world. We spent several years adjusting and making our family of four work. Then God did something else.

We received another opportunity to adopt a child. This time we were not thinking about it, planning it, or praying about another child. My sister called me one day and asked me if Roger and I would consider adopting another child. She proceeded to tell me her friend was pregnant but could not take care of another child. She did not feel comfortable considering anyone else. We were shocked and uncertain about what to do. We again went into prayer and a few weeks later, we decided to move forward with the adoption.

Having two daughters was amazing and terrifying at the same time. Learning how to navigate the adoption process and leaving the adoption open so that our daughter could someday meet her biological mother and be in contact with her grandparents and sibling were invigorating yet exhausting. Roger and I had a surplus of support and love throughout this process. There were times I second-guessed our decision because of the lengthy adjustment.

Then three years later, Roger and I adopted our youngest child, Rebekah. Her mother had four children and could not take care of Rebekah, so we were asked to adopt her. On the ultrasound, the fetus looked like a boy. We were excited to be expecting a boy, but here she appeared into the world as a girl, who we immediately loved, but we were not prepared for another girl. However, we were excited to be a family of five.

When we adopted Rebekah, it had been seven years since we had an infant in the home. Oh my goodness, I had forgotten how hard it was to care for an infant, but there we were, raising three daughters. The most important job in the world was pouring into three beautiful souls and helping them become amazing adults. I was even more determined to figure out life and to heal my heart. I worked hard to always put them first. It became especially important for me to strive to give my best in all that I did to heal, to learn, and to grow.

During this phase of my life, the entrepreneurial ideas and plans began developing out of my desire to become a better version of myself for my daughters. I also developed a love for motivational quotes, events, and anything I could get my hands on to help motivate me. It is amazing how your children can give you the motivation to be the best version of yourself. For the next twenty-plus years, Roger and I worked hard and dedicated our lives to pouring into our children. Was it perfect? No. Was it worth it? Yes. Roger and I always said our goal was to ensure our children elevated their lives higher than we did, and that is what they did.

Another goal for me as their mom was to heal my heart so that I could be healthy for them. I wanted to be present mentally and spiritually to help guide them through life. I know this sounds amazing and heroic, but it was the hardest thing I have ever done, being present and as mentally healthy as possible for our children. Managing church, marriage, motherhood, work, my relationship with God, and my relationships with my mother and father was so hard, but I knew it was necessary to get my life in order and to work on my mental health.

There were days when I wondered how I was going to make it. People ask me how I was doing it all. My response was always, "It's God, and I just get up every day and go, and just get it done."

My girls were and still are my everything; they are the reason I do what I do. I know I went a little overboard at times, but I would not change anything. Roger and I gave the girls everything we did not have and more. Sometimes, well maybe most of the time, I went overboard for their birthdays and everything else. The one thing I had to learn and to work through was my fear that what happened to me would happen to them as it relates to men. Therefore, my parenting out of fear caused several issues and arguments. I knew I had to overcome my fears, insecurities and unforgiveness, which took a long time. It affected my parenting when dealing with these issues. It took a while to recognize it and to see how it affected me as a mother. I was strict and overprotective, which led to many difficult conversations and disagreements. However, now that my daughters are all grown and successful, the challenges we had to overcome made it all worth it.

6

FORGIVING OTHERS - FORGIVING MYSELF

"I had to remind myself all the time to forgive myself and remember God forgave me and loved me."

-Shurvone

Having children changes you physically, mentally and emotionally. Children influence your overall outlook on life. When you are broken and confused from life experiences, having children motivates you to be the best version of yourself. You do everything to give them the best version of yourself. Your greatest hope is to help them develop into amazing human beings. I wanted to ensure my children's safety, love and protection, things I did not have as a child.

My children became my number one priority. Before motherhood, I did not realize how important it was for me to forgive others and myself. I did not realize how unforgiving I had become of others and myself. I was angry and felt robbed of the life I deserved. I was deprived of having a mother and a father, the vision of what I thought was normal. I guess once I became a mother and wife, I realized how much healing I had to do.

I had to forgive my mother and father for not being the parents I deserved. As I write these words, it makes me sad that I did not know better until I had kids. I cannot believe I carried the hurt and pain for so long. Roger helped me see the pain I was carrying and helped me acknowledge the hurt and anger in my heart. He pointed out I was always negative and irritated with my mother. I will never forget the question that changed me. Roger asked me why I was so mad at my mother. That is when I realized I had more work to do. I had to make a conscious decision to accept all the things I could not change and accept what I never would have.

I could not go back in time; my parents could not go back in time. I realized the process would be long once I accepted the fact I had to forgive; the first thing I did was have a conversation with my parents. It was terrifying and hard, but I got up the nerve to talk to them.

It was not a straightforward conversation about all the issues. My parents knew what happened and what did not happen. They knew they were absent. I know after they got their lives in order, it was a hard pill to swallow knowing the pain they caused. I could tell there was some guilt present when we spoke. Once we had a heart-to-heart conversation, I felt a sense of relief and peace.

However, much more work was necessary. I had to work on myself. Sometimes I had flashbacks or daydreams about what I lost in my childhood and I would lash out. I had to accept my parents could not provide the emotional love and support I needed if they did not know how. I had to accept I would never have the fairytale mother/father home life. As simple as this sentence is to write, it was one of the hardest things in my life to overcome.

I finally realized I could not move on or forward in my quest for healing without forgiving others and myself.

I also had to forgive every male that had ever hurt me or used me in some way. The most challenging part of my journey was forgiving myself for making decisions that affected my life negatively. Once I realized all my decisions were in response to my previous experiences in life, I was determined to change. I had to let go of doubt, fear and insecurity. I learned over the years what my triggers are and what takes me back down memory lane. However, as time went by, and I implemented my walk with God, prayer, and meditation, I lashed out less. I learned how to be more in tune with my feelings, my life, and my triggers. Then I had to learn what to do if I became triggered: take a walk, go into my room and shut the door, get in the shower, or be silent. My calming strategies did not always work. However, I never gave up and stopped trying to get it right. I also learned how to meditate and journal about my thoughts and feelings.

I do not think I ever told my father how I felt or allowed him to ask for forgiveness. However, I did spend a few memorable months with him before he passed. We spent time talking, praying, and reading the word, and the best thing of all was that I saw him attend church, accept the Lord into his life, and care for him until he passed. Being with him when he took his last breath was challenging but very special. It felt like a lifetime with him. God answered many years of prayers: to have my father accept Christ as his Lord and Savior. I waited all my life to see this, and God gave me a beautiful gift. God gave me time with my father that I will cherish forever: I had time to heal a lifetime of unforgiveness. I was at peace because God had answered my prayer.

Similarly, I was able to have a heart-to-heart with my mother and to share with her how her lifestyle had affected my life, and how hurt and angry I was for a long time. She asked me to forgive her, which I did at that moment, but I knew I had to work on not responding to my triggers. I went as far as having a conversation with Tommy and he apologized for introducing me to drugs and for almost ruining my life. These were all conversations that needed to happen to help me heal and grow. However, I had so much growing to do. I dealt with unforgiveness and still struggled with being a shy and insecure person. However, I was able to function, to elevate my nursing career, and to start multiple businesses. I always tried to improve myself, but I never felt as if I had arrived at a place where I was confident or bold enough to have a voice that made a difference. I am still in awe of how God guided me, groomed and protected me in my lowest of low.

Until you truly have forgiven those who hurt you,

including yourself, you do not realize how unforgiveness can affect the way you respond to people and to situations. When triggered by an event, praying and self-examination helped me calm down and assess what was upsetting to me at that moment. Another exercise I tried was asking myself what was so upsetting to me about the situation. I asked God to help me see people the way He saw them. Over time, I was able to manage my feelings toward the people who I needed to forgive. It was not always perfect, but I learned how to manage my triggers and feelings.

As an adult, I came to realize that forgiveness was mostly for my healing and getting unstuck from the past. I also believe that most people do things because of their environment or upbringing, and once you realize that, it helps you forgive others and yourself. Another long journey of traumatic events I had to forgive myself for was the multiple abortions I decided to have and allowing men to use and abuse my body.

I had to forgive myself for giving in to drug use. I had to forgive my parents for not protecting me. I had to forgive men for abusing me and for almost killing me with drugs. I had to forgive my grandfather for dying, which I know is strange, but I felt as if he had left me alone. I am sharing all these experiences so that you can see my healing was a difficult journey, but I made it and so can you. I encourage you to find what works for you if you still have to work through unforgiveness. Then, give yourself grace and time to heal as you walk through the process.

7

CONFIDENCE WITHOUT REGRET

"You need to be confident without regret." At that
moment, my life changed, and it hit me like a ton of
bricks. You are okay just the way you are; it is okay just
to be me. My journey to freedom began at that moment.
-Shurvone

As I sat in my counselor's beautiful, colorful, warm office waiting for our session to begin, I felt comfortable and safe. When I feel safe, it is easier for me to open up and to receive help. She filled her office with Disney characters, motivational quotes, and other feminine items that caught my eye and helped me relax. Our sessions usually began with small talk, we then dove into the work. This particular session; I wanted to talk about being overly concerned about what people thought of me and how I felt like that flaw held me back in life. I tried to get past those thoughts, but I could not figure out how. My counselor asked how do I think others see me. I easily could name ten positive attributes. When she asked how do I see myself, I could not share as many. Now that I think back, I did not feel confident or comfortable saying positive things about myself. It was easier to tell my counselor how I thought others perceived me. It is sad to think I was so insecure that I could not speak positively about myself. What I did not understand was how I could be so successful in my career yet so insecure. I hated being this way, and I wanted to change so bad. I felt trapped in my feelings. I could not figure out how to change. The struggle of wanting to change a behavior, but not knowing how is real. If you are in that situation and feel stuck don't give up. I chose to do whatever it took to change my life.

She turned around to the whiteboard and wrote, "you need to be confident without regret." At that moment, my life changed, and it hit me like a ton of bricks. I felt like crying. I do not know why God chose those words or that moment to reveal that it was okay just to be me. I guess I was ready to be free. I was tired of being tired. I wanted the freedom to be okay with who I was, with who I wanted to be, and with what I wanted to say without the concern of what others thought of me. My journey to freedom began at that moment. I wrote the words Confidence Without Regret in my journal at my desk. I remember thinking God was going to change my life using those words. I had no idea that it would be the title of my book seven years later. God will use everything in your life for his purpose, to heal you, change you and catapult you into your destiny. I remember being encouraged to be the best version of myself as a child. I was told I could be anything I wanted to be, constantly being reminded of how smart I was. My relatives and teachers also did their best to instill confidence and high self-esteem in me. However, along the journey of life, fear, self-doubt, low self-esteem, and low confidence became a struggle. It was a struggle to remember I was intelligent and capable of accomplishing my dreams. I hated being that way, but for some reason, I could not figure out how to be different or how to change. I had an internal struggle almost every day. The mind is quite an intriguing organ, and if you let it control you negatively, then you will be paralyzed mentally and will never live out your best life. This almost happened to me, but the "Never Give Up" mantra I developed saved my life at a young age.

Events in my early childhood changed me forever. When I was between four and five years old, I remember being a happy child living with my loving grandparents. I could be a kid and play and have fun. I remember not being afraid or timid. I simply felt safe and loved. However, all that changed when I was five years old. I remember being left in the foyer as if it were yesterday. I was fearful and lonely. It seemed like an eternity, standing there crying, not knowing what to do. The area seemed so big and dark. I did not know if it was daytime or evening. There was nothing or no one around me. How could I feel such loneliness at five years old?

How I can remember something that happened so many years ago is beyond me, but I know that experience impacted my future. I could not comprehend why I was being left again. I am told my father would visit me often. When he left, I would cry, so I assume this memory was possibly from one of his visits. For some reason, being alone and scared embedded itself into my soul and molded me into a shy little girl. That shy little girl lived in me throughout my adulthood. Every time I write about being home alone, I can feel the fear and loneliness. This experience embedded itself in my spirit, so much so that I was not comfortable doing things alone until I was in my thirties.

One other life-changing event happened when I was nine years old: my grandfather passed away. I remember the feeling of such a profound loss and a knowing in my soul that life would be different forever. I remember thinking I did not feel protected anymore. Another level of fear, insecurity, self-doubt, and low self-esteem set in. You might wonder how I felt that way being that I come from such a big family, but you do not know my family.

When you are young and specific experiences happen in your life, they form your opinions, thoughts, and world view, in turn, creating how you live your life. I became timid and did not talk much or make many friends after elementary school. I had a few neighborhood friends but no other friends from school. I attended four different high schools, so it was a chaotic time in my life. My mother and father would take turns deciding whether they wanted to care for me. When it did not work out, I ended up back at my grandmother's home. That part of my life is another book alone.

My first memory of being molested was at twelve years old, again at fifteen years old, then again at eighteen years old. I never reported it, and I never spoke of it, but I do not know why. Maybe it was fear. I do not know, but it haunted me for a long time. I allowed men to use and abuse my body. I understand that some of this might be hard to read, but I wanted to paint a clear picture of how my life and your life can be affected for years by the things that happen early in our lives. Now I know that I allowed men to abuse me because of my fears, insecurities, and the need to fill a void in my life. I had a false sense of safety and security.

I am not sure when I felt safe after my grandfather died. Remember I mentioned knowing my life would never be the same and not feeling protected after his death. It is crazy to think I knew these things, but I never would have imagined the life I had. I experienced many events in my life that produced additional fear and uncertainty—being a witness to physical abuse as well as drug and alcohol abuse and its horrific effect on my family. I experienced seeing someone overdose. Family events were ruined by the behaviors of someone addicted to drugs. I swore I would never become that person, a family member who used and abused drugs. These events further formed and solidified my fears, insecurities, and the need to feel safe. I looked in all the wrong places for that safety. I now know that the Holy Spirit was watching over me, guiding me, and protecting me. I made the wrong choices that could have and should have killed me.

During another vulnerable state of mind, I allowed my then-boyfriend to convince me to try drugs. All it took was one night, and I was hooked until I was a little over twenty years old. One night of stupidity led to two years of drug addiction. Until one morning, after being up all night, I heard the Holy Spirit say to me, "If you don't stop, you're going to die." I went cold turkey, never touching drugs again, never going to a group meeting for recovery. The desire and need for drugs just disappeared, and a few months later, I signed up for nursing school, not knowing it would change my life forever.

As strange as it sounds, I always would find a way to be strong in the face of adversity. Before I graduated from nursing school, I met and married a man who quickly became verbally and physically abusive. Again, the Holy Spirit protected me and helped me escape that marriage without any children or ties to the abuser. A few years later, I met and married my husband of twenty-eight years. As I advanced in my nursing career and marriage, I still struggled with many insecurities. I did not believe my husband loved me or could love a person like me. Oh boy, I put him through it because of my low self-esteem and zero confidence. Again, I found a way to push through it, to learn, and to persevere. I stood on "Never Give Up", God, and my mantra. I was tired of dealing with low self-esteem and low confidence.

As I advanced in my career, I tried my hand at many entrepreneurial endeavors, which led to a few ministry events. I believed I needed to do more work on myself because I still let people walk over me. I did not speak up for myself, I was exhausted. I was tired of feeling regret for not speaking up when I needed to. When I built up the courage to have a voice, it became easier to expand my voice in all areas of my life.

In the following pages, I will share some tools that will help you and guide you to develop your confidence and to live free of regret. My journey to freedom happened when I decided to face my fears and to do things that scared me and intimidated me. Each time I decided to face my fears and insecurities, I felt empowered. I have developed the skills and awareness that have helped me move quickly toward the fear with solutions and goals without being frozen. However, one thing is for sure: I will not let fear keep me from living in my purpose.

In this chapter, I am going to share life applications you can use to build your confidence and ultimately to change your life. You will gain clarity to focus on your purpose and to live free of regret. I am going to take you on a journey that will transform your thought process and help you take action to step into your purpose.

Regret is a sad and negative emotion. Even though we

know we cannot change the past, it can have a hold on our future if we do not move past it. If we do not know how to deal with regret in positive ways, then it can affect the rest of our lives in negative ways. I learned how to view my past as lessons, not regret. Your past creates your future. I believe everything we experience and the decisions we make shape us into the person we eventually become as adults. One of the best ways to make decisions you will not regret is to let your priorities guide you. Whenever faced with a decision, big or small, determine which option fits best with what is most important to you. Always keep in mind whatever decision you make has the power to change your life forever.

The option that is most closely in alignment with your beliefs, priorities and values will likely be the best decision for YOU. Do not worry about what others think is best—their opinion comes from their wants and needs. Always choose according to your priorities. Using this strategy to make decisions and living with your choices help you live with no regrets. Even if things do not go as planned, you can be confident you made the right decision for yourself based on your own needs and priorities. Let's explore how to determine your priorities.

Oftentimes, a decision can be complicated by several factors you might consider necessary. Of course, each option leans differently and might cause confusion and uncertainty. So, what do you do?

Follow this three-step strategy to cut out the confusion, to discover your priorities, and to make decisions you can trust:

1. **Reflect.** Think about what is most important to you and write a list.
   - Your spouse, family, and other loved ones
   - Your faith
   - Your dreams and goals
   - Your ethics and morals
   - Your health
   - Your work
   - Other things of importance to you

2. **Arrange.** Please put the list in order with the essential items at the top.

Some of your most important priorities will change at different times in your life. For example, if you are going to college to get a degree, then completing your education may be more critical than your part-time job. However, when you are the sole provider for your family, your job is one of your top priorities.

3. Refer to your priority list when making choices.

Make decisions toward the option that provides an advantage for the items at the top of your list. You will rarely regret making choices according to your higher priorities. Focus on making the right decision based on your priorities, then trust yourself to do what is needed to make your decision a reality.

You can avoid most regrets simply by living on purpose. What does that mean? You *choose* a life of joy then actively pursue that life. Spend your time making the memories that you *want* to have. No one has ever gone to their grave wishing they had spent *more* time working or watching TV. The secret to avoiding regret is to do what matters most. In other words, take action to create the life you want. Do not spend your time mourning your current situation and wishing for more. Instead, do something *every day* to bring the life you desire into your present and to exhibit the qualities you want. Sooner than you realize, your dreams will become your reality, and you will have thoroughly enjoyed the journey, too!

ELIMINATING PAST REGRETS

When you harbor resentment about the past, it only

hurts you. Nothing good comes from regret or the negative emotions that accompany it.

Here are some techniques that can help you overcome your feelings of regret:

- Things that happened in the past cannot be changed no matter how hard we try or how much time we spend wishing they had happened differently. If there is a way to make amends, then do it and move on with your life. Focus on your present, look forward to your future, and leave the past in the past.
- When you live in the moment, you are entirely focused on the now. You feel the moment's joys, pleasures and sensations and appreciate them. The more you practice this technique, the more you can tune out everything and embrace this moment.
- Affirmations can help you change your mindset from feeling sad about the past to accepting it so that you can live a more joyful life. They are positive statements that you can repeat every time a regretful thought presents itself.

Here are some examples of affirmations:

- I let go of my regret to make room for joy.
- I am happy with who I am now and look forward to a positive future.
- I live each day with gratitude for the precious gift of life.
- Meditation helps you envision your life without regret. Watch the negative feelings dissipate in the clear air around you – gone forever, never to return!

HOW TO REGAIN CONFIDENCE AFTER YOU HAVE FACED CHALLENGES IN YOUR LIFE

It is common to feel as if your confidence has vanished after you have faced some difficult challenges in life. Do you know how to rebuild your self-confidence? Don't know what to do to regain your confidence? If so, then this information will be helpful for you.

To boost your self-confidence, consider these tips:

Know who you are. When you reconnect with the person you are deep down, your confidence will begin to rise again.

- Practice self-reflection to figure out what

kind of person you are. Think about your inner self to discover your strengths.

- Take time to become clear about the amazing person you are today.

Acknowledge the phenomenal people in your life. Think of your friends. Consider the close relationships you enjoy with your family members. Perhaps you are cultivating friendships with co-workers you respect and admire.

Stay connected in your love life. When you are emotionally close and intimately involved with your partner, you do not feel alone. You have a sense that, "Together, we can overcome anything." Knowing that makes you feel stronger as an individual.

Embrace challenges. Tell yourself, "I don't know for sure if I can succeed, but I do know for sure that I will try my hardest." Build your confidence by accepting new challenges.

- Whenever you experience a challenge, you learn something you can apply later in life.

Avoid comparing yourself to others. Comparing yourself to others sets you up for failure. The answer to

"Why can't I be pretty *and* smart like Jen?" is, "Because you're not Jen—you're you!"

- When you compare yourself to others, especially when you are searching for your confidence, you might feel as if you always come out with the short end of the stick.
- Identify your strengths and build on them. You do not have to be the same as everyone else. Acknowledge the positive attributes you possess. *Recognize your strengths.*

Establish new goals. What is it you hope to accomplish in your life? Whatever it is that you seek, it is important. Write new goals to help you get excited about your future and focus on moving forward.

Work toward your goals to achieve them. As you accomplish things you have worked hard for, you will feel as if you can do anything. You will experience deep feelings of satisfaction and confidence as you put your efforts into things that matter to you.

- Working toward a goal and achieving it are some of the sweeter things in life. Welcome to the process!

Use positive self-talk. Speak to yourself using phrases, such as "I know I can do it," "I did a fantastic job," "It's time to go for it!", "Never Give Up", and "You got this".

- Talk to yourself as if you are the smartest, kindest, most talented person you have ever met.
Be positive, self-supporting, and honest with yourself. You will be stunned at the difference it will make in your life when you speak positively to yourself.

Working to regain your confidence is an exciting, enlightening, and worthwhile process.

You will begin to believe in yourself again. Recite the following affirmations. These are affirmations I have tried, implemented, and incorporated into my life. If you think you cannot implement these affirmations at once, then tackle them two or three at a time.

These steps will be second nature in no time. Self-reflection helps you heal and grow.

1. I believe in myself and in my abilities. I think positively. I remember that hard times are temporary. I control how I react to external circumstances. I look for ways to use any situation to my advantage. I am creative and

flexible.

2. I focus on my strengths and achievements. I take pride in my accomplishments.

3. I stand tall. Looking confident helps me feel surer of myself. I hold my head up and make eye contact.

4. I stay calm under pressure. When I feel tense, I take a few deep breaths and stretch my muscles. I slow down so that I can think clearly and review my options. I relax with a warm bath or a cup of tea.

5. I advocate for my needs. I stand up for my principles.

6. I continue to learn and to grow. I enjoy gaining new skills and knowledge that strengthen my professional qualifications and enrich my personal life.

7. I built a strong network of support. I can count on my family and friends for practical assistance, comfort and reassurance.

8. I invest in myself. I love and accept myself as I am. I embrace my feelings and validate my experiences. I look after my mental, physical and spiritual needs.

9. I act. I tackle challenges rather than overanalyze them. Making an effort and seeing results boosts my faith in myself.

10. Today, I exude confidence. I rid myself of doubts and fears. I can overcome life's challenges and reach my goals.

Commit to yourself, always value your own opinion, and never give up on your dreams and goals. No matter how many times you fall, get up and keep going. Trying again and again is better than never taking a chance. Keep going. You got this!

8

IT'S OK TO START OVER

Never compare your journey with someone. God gave the vision to you.

-Shurvone

How many times have you started over? How many times did you feel scared when you had to start over? How many times did you think, What am I going to do? How am I going to get through this?

I have started over many times in my life, and each time it was scary. I felt insecure and unsure of what I needed to do. When I say it was scary, it was not always an unpleasant situation. It was scary most times because of the unknown or because it was not a change

I initiated. I want to share a few life-changing events in my life when I started over and had to pick myself up and keep going. Those times were never easy; however, that internal drive and determination kept me going.

When change presents itself, it can be unnerving at times, specifically when it is related to a career, a big move, or a change in a relationship, but I have always been able to pivot. When a change was thrown at me unexpectedly, I felt out of control and lost, not knowing what to do.

The first big change was starting over when my mother decided it was time to care for me, my sister, and my brother. It is strange to me that I cannot remember certain details about this move. I believe God wanted to protect me; therefore, part of my memory is missing. No matter how hard I try to remember certain details, I cannot recall them. I believe it is a blessing to have certain memories erased. There were so many events that sent me on a different journey; however, God did not let me remember and experience everything that happened to me.

I do not remember the actual transition from my grandmother's home to my mother's home. I remember seeing this big house with a beautiful yard. The inside of the home was immaculate. I remember being excited to have my own room. I felt joy and excitement knowing that we would be living with our mother and be a family. This was the first time in my young life that I lived with my mother, sister, and brother all at the same time in one home. It felt so good to be in a normal family, or what I thought was a normal family. The joy of having a home and of living with my mother and siblings was amazing.

However, this amazing feeling, the safe home environment, and the feeling of having a family did not last long. I do not remember moving out. I just remember one day we went from being in a safe place to being scared and uncertain of our future. I was in the seventh grade, probably twelve years old, and still shy, so again I just went with the flow of things. I know now it was God keeping me and protecting my mind from my fears, being sad and afraid. One day, we were a family and what felt like the next day, we all were separated again, and I was back at my grandmother's home. This back-and-forth scenario, living with my mother then going back to my grandmother's home, happened several times until I became an adult.

Because of these life experiences, I subconsciously was trained to deal with transition and change no matter how hard or scary it was. I also realize where my internal fight to never give up came from, a spirit of constantly looking for ways to figure out how to make things work and how to pivot when faced with adversity. You might be wondering how I learned to navigate adversity and what tools and strategies I used to overcome it. Again, I realize now it was God guiding me and developing what people call a strong intuition or discernment. I always knew things in my life would be okay, not always knowing how. God has always been my source and guidance even when I did not realize it.

As I grew older, I developed a powerful desire and motivation to take care of myself. I will never forget getting my first job at seventeen. I felt proud but scared at the same time. I was able to purchase my own car and to buy all the things I needed for my final year of high school. It was a proud moment but also a sad moment because I missed the traditional family unit. I missed my parents taking me shopping, dropping me off at work, or waiting for me to come home. I craved those warm family moments, but I knew they were not coming, so I did what I had to do. I am still amazed at how I figured things out. I realized my shyness was how I protected myself.

I had my extended family and my grandmother's love, but as a young woman, I wanted my mother, my father, and the whole family unit. Why am I sharing this portion of my life? What does it have to do with starting over? I wanted to share this portion of my life so that you know you are not alone. So many times in life, we fear starting over. We feel like failures, or we simply feel lost. Give yourself permission to start over.

It is okay to start over and to regroup when life presents overwhelming challenges or when you simply want change. Starting over can be exciting. I do not want you to think all change is scary. I have experienced exciting changes. Becoming a mother, getting married, and starting a business were changes I was eager to make. I welcomed those changes with open arms. Whenever I was presented with an opportunity for change, I always did my best to adapt by implementing a plan to make things better. I must be honest; I did not always rise to the occasion. It was a process. I also started over many times in relationships, careers, and my entrepreneurial endeavors. So don't ever be afraid to start over. Never regret it, always use the experiences as an opportunity to learn.

9

THE BUTTERFLY EXPERIENCE

"All butterflies represent our life's transformation. When we grow and evolve, the process of changing from a caterpillar to a butterfly is very symbolic of what can happen when we actively pursue our purpose."

-Shurvone

During the years of my struggles with low self-esteem and low confidence, I managed to start many businesses because of my entrepreneurial drive and motivation. However, I was never passionate about what I was doing because I was not doing what I wanted to do. That never stopped me. I tried it all: Avon, Tupperware, Princess House, Mary Kay, three different jewelry companies, and probably a few more. I finally settled on my own gift basket and t-shirt business. It was quite successful, and I enjoyed making the baskets and t-shirts. I just did not have the voice to get what I needed to sustain the business. I was too shy, overly concerned about what people thought of my business, so eventually I closed the business.

However, as I have mentioned, I always had a "Never Give Up" attitude and would try anything to improve. In my mind and heart, I wanted to improve but could not build the courage to do so. I felt defeated, frustrated, and trapped. As a believer in God, I did pray and I knew God protected me, but I did not trust God enough to believe that he could heal ME. It took many years to realize I had profound trust issues and I did not trust God. It was another hurdle I had to conquer to walk in my purpose, to gain the confidence to do what I was placed on this planet to do. As I worked through my challenges, I came to learn what worked for me. I learned I needed quiet time. I had to learn to trust God, and for me that meant knowing God and trusting my relationship with Him was just that: "mine". I had to let go of what other people thought of my walk with God. It is crazy how I let my whole life be controlled by the fear of what people thought of me. The reason I did not trust God is because I did not trust anyone at the time, including myself.

During the process I call the Cocoon, I was determined to change. I began reading books by Joyce Myers, Sarah Young and Napoleon Hill. I surrounded myself with motivational quotes. I began meditating, and that is when my life drastically changed because I finally learned how to slow my thoughts down, how to calm myself when I became nervous or scared. I finally reached a place in my life where I was tired of being tired. I was tired of looking at people passing me up and getting what they wanted in life. I wanted to be free and to receive what I wanted out of life.

The life cycle of a butterfly represents the transformation I experienced. My experiences climaxed when I felt as though I had accepted my whole being, my calling, and my purpose. One night in February of 2021, I had a vivid dream of a beautiful butterfly on my back. It was very colorful, and it flapped its wings. It did not scare me or seem creepy. It was simply beautiful. I had no idea what this dream meant, or how it would change my life.

Many people remain in the caterpillar phase, never wanting to or knowing how to wake up to their true purpose. It takes courage to confront self-doubt and completely change who you are. You must be still, wrap yourself in a cocoon, and stabilize your core so that you have firm ground to launch from.The cocoon represents meditation, prayer, stillness, trust and wisdom. When you emerge from that cocoon, you are awake and enlightened to your true purpose. Little did I know that walking in my boldness and freedom would be the launching pad for this book. Through the process, I gained the courage to shave my head, which led to me learning I had alopecia and connecting with women across the country who deal with alopecia.

When I decided to shave my head, I immediately felt beautiful, and not once since I shaved my head have I regretted it. I was officially diagnosed with traction alopecia from damaged hair follicles due to wearing wigs and other hairstyles that stressed my hair. Embracing it helped me achieve freedom and purpose.

I could not hide behind hair anymore, which represented freedom, no fear, no shame, and full acceptance of my being. It took me a few months to understand the deep feeling of peace I had about being bald.

For me, it was the most vulnerable thing I ever could have done. I shaved my head and did not wear a wig. It was bold and beautiful at the same time. I knew I had to come to terms with myself, with being bold, with speaking my mind, and with being confident and unapologetic. I finally had busted out of the cocoon and was ready to fly. I was ready to step into my purpose. I decided to share my story to help others walk in their purpose and never give up on their dreams no matter what. It took most of my adult life to feel comfortable, fearless and safe. As I have mentioned before, I now realize that God always has been with me and guided me.

When I finally accepted myself, my life, my journey and all my flaws, I truly believe that is why I became the butterfly(metaphorically). I was not afraid to shine. I was not afraid to fly and to be all that I can be. It is not a perfect road, but it is my road and my journey. I want to encourage anyone reading this to embrace your life to the fullest and to try what works for you. Look for those things in your life you need to heal and for whatever tools you need to help you along the way. In this book, I provide tools and suggestions to help you along. Remember, when things don't always work out the first time, do not quit. Keep going until you find your groove.

10

WALKING IN YOUR PURPOSE

*"Never give up on your dreams, God has a plan
and purpose for your life."*

-Shurvone

In this chapter, you will have an opportunity to walk through these guides, suggestions, and tools to help you walk in your purpose. Walking in your purpose is scary at times because not everyone will understand you or support you, but you must believe in your dreams and vision more than anyone else. I hope the suggestions and tools below will help you and bless you to walk boldly.

DISCOVERING YOUR LIFE'S PURPOSE

There is a purpose for your life, whether you believe it or not. You may have to take several paths, but with a little redirection, you can find where you are meant to be.

The first clue to figuring out your purpose in life is to consider what natural abilities, gifts and talents you were born with. Ask yourself the following questions:

- Are you artistic or musical?
- Is it easy for you to talk to people?
- Are you a natural communicator?
- Do you love to socialize?
- Do you love to decorate and rearrange your home?
- Are you good at taking charge?
- Are you creative and crafty?
- Do you understand electronics and technical gadgets?
- Do you understand computer technology?
- Do people compliment you on your style?
- Are you a good writer?
- Do you have good organizational skills?

Once you figure out your natural talents, you can figure

out what you are supposed to do with those gifts and talents. This is your purpose in life.

WHAT DO YOU LOVE TO DO?

Have you ever sat down and really reflected on what you love to do?

There are millions of possibilities, so start with the gifts and talents you were born with. From there, figure out what you love to do that requires using those gifts and talents.

- If you are artistic or musical, then teaching others how to draw, paint, or play an instrument may be your calling in life.
- Being naturally social, you might consider being an organizer for social events.
- If you are always redecorating and rearranging your home, then why not get paid to do it and start an interior decorating business?
- Being a natural-born leader opens all kinds of doors that could lead you in many different directions. Does your church or other
- Do local community groups need someone to head up a department? You may find your

purpose there.

- If you are good at making crafty things, then volunteering at a preschool or elementary school may be fulfilling for you. Using your creative ability could open the door to a career in graphic arts as well.
- If you are technically inclined, then perhaps you might consider fixing equipment, or you might enjoy working in an electronics store.
- If you have a strong knowledge of computers, then you are certain to find a career online or with a high-tech company, or you might even consider starting your own business.
- If you are naturally stylish and love to keep up with what is new in the fashion world, then perhaps designing your own line of clothing or accessories is your purpose. Or maybe you would enjoy helping others discover what style works best for them by working in a clothing store. Another option may be to offer your services as a fashion consultant to those who are unemployed so that they can learn how to dress professionally for job interviews.
- The love of writing may be something you do not even realize yet. With blogging becoming

the most popular way to market a business, getting paid to write is a great way to make money from home. Many people have started a simple blog that has turned into a money-making machine. Begin by writing on topics you already have knowledge about and go from there. You might be surprised at how much money you can make with your love of writing.

- Using your organizational skills, you might be fond of preparing homes to be sold or of helping elderly persons organize their homes. You also could offer your services online as an organizational consultant or teach those who are not naturally organized.

Finding your purpose in life simply takes self-reflection as well as some trial and error. Free yourself from wandering through life without purpose. We are all here for a reason. Once you find your purpose and begin living it, you will be happy and fulfilled.

7 WAYS TO DISCOVER YOUR LIFE PURPOSE

There are several avenues to explore when it comes to discovering your life purpose. Unfortunately, no one else can find it for you. Because your life purpose is unique from anyone else's, it is a mission that you—and only you—can complete.

In your quest for passion, concentrate on enjoying the journey itself. When you stop stressing about your life's purpose, it sometimes falls into your lap.

Here are some ways you can discover your life purpose:

1. **Write about how you feel.** Try journaling with a pen and paper or grab your laptop and just start writing. Write about how you truly feel and what you want out of life. Remember that no one is going to read this other than you, so do not be afraid to express your thoughts.

- Go back and reread your journal entries every so often. Many times, reflecting presents new realizations that you did not think of when you wrote your entries.

2. **Pursue your passions.** If you are passionate about a certain subject, then maybe you can make a career or hobby out of it so that you can.

3. **Engage in activities that are personally meaningful to you.** This way, each day of your life will feel like it matters, and you will have a life purpose.

- Consider your talents. Think about the areas

in which you naturally excel to see if you can turn these skills into something meaningful for you.

- Many people are drawn to a life purpose that makes them feel as though they are making a true difference in the lives of other people. If this fits you, then you will be fulfilled through helping others in need.
- For example, if you find that you are good at comforting people, then perhaps you should consider a career as a counselor.

4. **Converse with inspiring people.** Strike up a conversation with someone who inspires you. While you might not be interested in the same things, you can talk about how they discovered their life purpose. Their triumphs and struggles will make good lessons for you in your journey to your purpose.

5. **What brings you joy?** Reflect on the moments in your life when you are most happy. What are you doing at these times? You can begin the quest for your life purpose by using what already makes you happy. Remember that you are not necessarily searching for something exotic. After all, your life purpose may be right under your nose.

6. **Embrace change.** Sometimes the thing that holds you

back from self-discovery is a fear of change. Not only is there comfort and safety in not taking risks, but you also may never discover your life's true purpose. Learn to embrace change because life is constantly changing.

7. **Walking in Your Purpose.** Everyone has a set of values they adhere to in life. You can use your values as a starting point to discover your life purpose. Make a list of your values with your most important ones at the top. If you think about what you can do to honor those values in life every day, then you may find your purpose.

Finding your purpose in life may not be as hard as you think. Use these strategies on your journey and one day soon you will realize you have found the one feature of your life that makes everything worthwhile.

ADD PURPOSE TO YOUR LIFE WITH THESE STRATEGIES

A person without a purpose is usually not happy or content. They are constantly looking for excuses to justify not doing anything with their lives. They do not have any direction because they think the world owes them something.

NO ONE SETS OUT TO LIVE

A LIFE WITHOUT A PURPOSE.

You know you lack a sense of purpose when you do not feel satisfied with what you have and are always looking for more, even though you do not realize it.

So, how can you break the cycle of a lack of purpose? Try these strategies:

1. **Take a well-deserved break.** Having a break from your daily life can do wonders for your mood. When you do not feel like doing anything, you might be burned out or just stressed. A break helps recharge your batteries and gives you a new perspective.

- Give yourself a mental health day. On the said day, decide to let go of what you think you are supposed to do and focus on what makes you happy.
- Many people believe that success is just outside our comfort zone. That may be true in some circumstances. But when you are in a cycle of a lack of purpose, a good break is just what you need to recharge your batteries.
- Taking a break can allow you to discover your true purpose in life. You will feel motivated to do more.

2. **Follow things that interest you.** Many people have interests they would like to pursue but do not. They ignore those interests because it seems like a waste of time.

- The truth is, stringing together your hobbies and interests can help you discover your purpose.
- For example, if you love video games, then try building an online video game store using Shopify and start selling video games.
- If you love jewelry, then start a jewelry business online. If you love photography, then create your own photography business. And if you love graphic design, then design business cards, brochures, and other materials.
- That is not to say your purpose needs to relate to money. It should relate to something you are passionate about. You want a purpose that excites you.

3. **Admit that you are stuck.** The thing with getting stuck in a cycle is that you do not notice it. The feelings slowly build up, and before you know it, you have become apathetic. You begin feeling as if everything you do is just killing time.

- Then those feelings turn into anxiety, depression, and discouragement. Regardless of how hard you try; the cycle keeps repeating itself. Do not blame yourself for feeling the way you do.
- The loop will not change until you recognize it for what it is. Once you do, you can break it for good.

4. **Follow artistic endeavors.** Many people turn to art as a way of expressing their feelings. Writing poetry, painting, or sculpting can help you unlock feelings you were too afraid to feel.

- When you express those emotions, you will break that cycle and feel more passionate about things in your life.
- Exercising your artistic side also helps because physical activity makes you feel better, giving you more purpose.
- The goal is not to sell your works of art or to make a name for yourself but to enjoy yourself.

5. **Do not hesitate to speak to others.** The pandemic has made it difficult to move freely and to interact with

friends and loved ones. If you are feeling isolated, then try reaching out to someone, even if only by phone.

Finding your purpose is essential to living a life that pleases you. It is not uncommon to get lost in life by your circumstances. While feeling this way can be discouraging, it does not have to be. There are ways to overcome it by finding purpose in your life.

11

OVERCOMING LOW SELF-ESTEEM, BEING CONFIDENT, AND LIVING IN YOUR PURPOSE

In this chapter, I will give you practical tips, tools, and action items you can implement into your life and the journey to becoming confident. One of the best ways to fill your life with passion is to live in the present moment. Living with total focus will take some practice because it differs from the mindset you may be used to. But with time, when you continue focusing on what you want your life to look like, transformation will happen. Are you ready for transformation?

Follow these tips to help you experience present moment living:

1. Heed the opportunity of this moment. Opportunities are all around you each day. Keep your mind open to opportunities that can benefit you and take advantage of them while they are right in front of you.

2. Stay focused. When distracting thoughts try to take you away from this very moment, regain your focus by consciously asking yourself these questions:
- Where am I? (Here)
- What time is it? (Now)
- What am I thinking about? (Only what I am doing at this moment)

The questions above will help you put your worries and distractions aside. If necessary, tell yourself that you will simply think about them at another time but not right now. If you do this enough, then you will find that it becomes easier and easier to keep your focus.

GO FOR IT AND GIVE IT ALL YOU'VE GOT

When you put your best efforts into any endeavor, it is

hard not to walk in your purpose. If you are going to do something, then it is worth doing well. No wishy-washy efforts for you!

Letting your passion shine through in all your actions makes everything you do in your life worthwhile.

Use these tips to help you boost your purpose:

1. **Determine your priorities.** When you know without a doubt what is most important to you, you can make choices and decisions with confidence. Choose the option that is most conducive to your higher priority, and you will be inspired to go full force with your decision.

2. **Live on purpose.** Living on purpose is choosing your own life according to your priorities. Simplify your life: include in your schedule only those things that are important to you.

3. **Clarify your goals.** Know exactly what you want and how you are going to get there.

4. **Divide your goals into achievable steps and focus on completing one step at a time.** Rejoice as you achieve each step because you are one step closer to your goal. This will inspire you and build momentum.

5. **Believe in yourself.** Nothing helps you go full force like confidence. The first three steps above will help you gain confidence in yourself. Trust yourself and you will find the purpose you have been seeking.

BE OPTIMISTIC

An important part of a passionate mindset is an optimistic attitude. When you think positive thoughts, the passion to pursue something comes easily.

On the other hand, if you are having second thoughts or negative feelings, then it is hard to be passionate about it. There is no benefit to doing something halfheartedly. What kind of attitude is that? Do you see how it can kill your passion? It does not even make much sense when you look at it logically, but that is the way we are sometimes. Our fears do not always make sense.

You will find that you most often get what you expect. If you expect good things, then that is the way events in your life usually turn out. An optimistic attitude leads to choices that bring you what you desire.

Even when you are faced with challenges, you tend to discover the silver lining or to find a workable solution if you are optimistic. Optimism keeps you fired up and moving in a direction that makes you happy.

With optimism, you can find the opportunities in your challenges. When life hands you lemons, you can make lemonade—and like it!

You can foster an optimistic attitude by:

1. Using positive self-talk and affirmations to replace negative thoughts

2. Meditating daily to visualize the life you desire and inspire yourself toward action

3. Asking yourself: Why not? What if it does work? How can I make this possible?

TAKE ACTION

Passion is incomplete without action. Become the most action-oriented person you know. Learn to take swift and decisive action to take advantage of opportunities. The only way you can make your dreams come true is by acting. Otherwise, a dream is just a dream.

Rather than sitting around thinking how nice it would be "if . . .", find a way to make it happen. Create a plan and go for it.

Instead of wasting time worrying about the scary "what ifs", make the best plan you can then implement it to bring the best scenario to fruition.

When a challenge enters your path, seek a solution to get around it, then take action to continue moving forward.

Action fuels your passion! You will find that the more you take action to get what you want, the more passionate you will feel about it.

LEARN SOMETHING NEW EVERY DAY

Another way to spark your passion is to acquire additional knowledge and to develop new skills. While learning about new things, you may find something you are excited about.

Here are some ways you can discover new passions:

1. **Pursue a new hobby.** Is there something you have always wanted to try? Now's the time!

2. **Take a class.** Look into your community or school district's programs for interesting subjects.

3. **Travel.** Whether in your own city or in a foreign land, traveling can lead to exciting passions.

4. **Read books.** Whether fiction or fact-based, books introduce you to entirely new perspectives, cultures, ideas, etc.

5. **Surf the Net.** You can learn about anything on the Internet: facts, news, and innovative ideas. Just make sure the sources are credible and the information is accurate. Not everything online is true.

When you learn something new every day, you gain a wealth of knowledge that keeps your mind active and processing new ideas. Rarely will you feel stagnant. Instead, you will be more likely to find a plethora of new passions you never knew existed.

STEP OUTSIDE YOUR COMFORT ZONE

In venturing outside of our comfort zones, we expand our horizons. Our world suddenly becomes much bigger, opening the doors to a vast array of new possibilities. With new possibilities come new opportunities and—you guessed it—a new passion.

Outside your comfort zone, you will be able to take actions you were afraid of, reach for dreams that you forbid yourself from working toward, and allow yourself the pride and joy of achieving the success you deserve. Stepping outside your comfort zone will be uncomfortable at first, but once you get used to doing it, you will wonder how you could have kept yourself so confined before.

A good way to get acclimated to the change is to do it little by little. Try simple things like taking a different route to work or trying different ethnic restaurants.

Think of life as a great adventure and wake up each day anticipating the exciting adventures of the day ahead. Every day, have a new experience to expand your horizon a little beyond where it was yesterday. Try one new thing, make one new call, meet one new person, and so on.

Soon you will be used to new experiences and know they usually turn out good. With your unfailing optimism, you will be ready to take that leap of faith to rekindle lost dreams and long-forgotten passions and claim them with mighty action.

GIVE THANKS

Feeling gratitude for your blessings—and showing it—helps bring out your passion. When you feel greatly blessed, it is hard not to feel passionate about your life. It also attracts better things for you to be grateful for.

When you awake, give thanks for all the good things coming in the day ahead. When you retire at night, give thanks for the blessings you received throughout the day.

In between, say "thank you" to everyone who brightens your day. From your child who hugged you, to the stranger who opened a door for you, let them know you are thankful for what they did.

Expressing your gratitude not only makes others feel better, and more apt to help you again, but also makes you feel better. It adds one more measure of joy to your day.

FIND A CAREER THAT EXCITES YOU

Are you happy with your career? If not, then perhaps it is not the right one for you. For most of us, a good portion of our lives are spent at our workplace. Our job has much to do with our overall feelings of success. Therefore, we must enjoy what we do for a living.

If you do not like your job, then how can you be passionate about succeeding in it?

Can you imagine spending your time doing something you are passionate about and making a living from it?

This is not only possible, but you also will enjoy much greater success following this path.

In pursuing interests that please you, not only will you have the passion that drives you to excellence in your field, but also the enthusiasm will be contagious. Your enthusiasm can convert prospects into clients and attract co-operation from business associates. Your passion also can propel you over hurdles by encouraging you to seek solutions and to take appropriate action.How do you design your career around your passions?

These tips can help you bring your passions into your career:

1. **Determine your passions.** Oftentimes, a career can be enjoyable even if it is not related to your most passionate hobbies. What do you enjoy doing? Meeting people? Working alone? Traveling in your work?

- Seek out work opportunities that cater to what you like to do.
- Take a career aptitude test to guide you to new ideas and opportunities.

2. **Consider your own business.** You can start by offering your own products and services part-time. Once you have built your business income up to your

current level of income, you can transition into full-time.

- If you decide to start your own business, then create a plan to address these items:
- What are the costs to start and attain all supplies needed? How can you get these funds together? From savings? With a loan? How will you repay it?
- Research what you need to learn about having your own business. Paperwork and taxes can be a passion-killer if you have not done your homework or hired an expert to take care of those things.
- Prepare ahead of time by finding a mentor.
- Develop the skills you need to succeed. If it takes further education or practice, then make it happen.
- Acquire appropriate licenses or certifications.
- How will you market your business?
- Determine your USP. Your USP is your unique selling point. How will you be different (and better) than other businesses in your field? Will you offer bonuses? Fanatical customer service?
- You must establish yourself as unique to

stand out from the competition.

The possibilities are endless when you allow your passions to drive your career. Do your research and execute. You will be glad you did.

SHOW YOUR LOVE

Love is one of our greatest passions. The big secret to feeling more passion in your relationship is to demonstrate more passion yourself. Show your partner your gratitude, love and respect for all they do. The more you show it, the more your partner reciprocates, and the more passion ignites in both of you.

Always be honest with your partner and listen to their point of view to avoid misunderstandings. Honesty is always the best policy.

Be affectionate and playful. Some think relationships are all work, but they are just the opposite. When it is fun being around each other, your passion comes alive, and you naturally want to make each other happy.

When you have a difference of opinion, remember that you genuinely love this person. This person is the most important person in your life. This simple point keeps you from saying things you will regret later, helps you be more patient, and enables win-win compromises.

DREAM BIG DREAMS

An important strategy to create more passion in your life is to dream big. How can you even desire to accomplish great things if you limit yourself to small dreams?

Bigger dreams carry greater passion. They get you more excited about the possibilities that await you if you make them come true.

So, dream big dreams then follow the techniques you have learned in this book to ignite your passions and to bring you the life you have always wanted—a life filled with passion.

YOU ARE GOOD ENOUGH

One of the most common self-critical thoughts is that you are not enough. It can stem from comparative and internalized criticism.

How can you change the "I'm not enough" mentality?

Understand where these negative thoughts come from and how to reframe them:

1. **Why do you feel as if you are not enough?** The first step is to get to the root of this thought.

- Examine your feelings and consider your past.
- Why do you feel you are never enough, and where do these feelings come from?

2. **Believing you are enough may require healing the past.**

3. **If you are having difficulty letting go of this self-criticism,** then counseling or therapy may help you get past these thoughts.

- Try journaling, meditation, or other contemplative activities to release the things that are holding you back.

4. **Say, "I am good enough."** Each time this negative thought comes up, rephrase it to a thought that uplifts you and makes you feel as though you are good enough. Remember that you are unique with your own special combination of gifts and talents.

- In many cases, the roots of this self-critical thought can be found in the past. Difficult childhoods, dysfunctional families, illnesses, and traumas can make you feel less worthy.

5. **Remember it is an internal message.** Even if others are praising you and complimenting you, you may feel as if you are not enough. This happens because negative thinking is an internal mindset that is hard to shed.

- Remind yourself that you are enough. You are smart enough, strong enough, and good enough to do anything. You are capable of remarkable things and can accomplish what you desire.

Once you realize your past may be controlling your present, it becomes easier to reframe this self-critical mindset.

"I'LL NEVER IMPROVE"

When you are stuck and have not reached your goals, it is common to believe you will never improve.

You may think you will never get better and never get past a certain point.

However, the "I'll never improve" mentality can hold you back. It can make you give up on your dreams and make you walk away from potential opportunities.

It is important to reframe this self-critical thought. If you do not, then it will make life more stressful.

Give it time. Give yourself enough time to strengthen your skills in the area or topic you are working on. Do not judge the process.

Say, "I'm learning and getting better." Reframe the self-critical talk by reminding yourself that you are always learning.

Another way to fight self-criticism is to say, "I'm good enough now."

You also can say, "I'm getting better all the time."

Saying these new phrases will help you feel more optimistic about what you are struggling to learn and boost your self-esteem.

You can eliminate self-criticism by putting less pressure on yourself. You are more likely to be critical of yourself when you expect too much, even if the expectations are realistic. Give yourself a break. Be patient with yourself and feel good about learning something new.

11 WAYS TO ELEVATE YOUR CONFIDENCE

Confidence grows through a series of experiences and challenges over your lifetime. Each day, you are given several opportunities to build your confidence through difficult conversations, stressful moments, and uncomfortable situations. It is your reaction to these opportunities that determines your courage, resolve and strength. Through practice and preparation, you can elevate your confidence. Get in a quiet space and spend some time pondering, reading, and writing your responses to the questions below.

1. What can I do to boost my confidence in how I look and feel?
2. How does my body language paint a vivid picture of my confidence?
3. What positive affirmations and motivational quotes do I live by?
4. What are my goals for this week, month, and year?
5. Who is important in my life? Do I treat them with an abundance of love and kindness?
6. When I reflect on my life, what are my successes? How can I improve?
7. What am I passionate about?
8. Who and what am I grateful for? Why?

9. How do I challenge myself to go outside of my comfort zone?
10. What do I have to celebrate today?
11. When the going gets tough, how do I react?

Finding your life purpose can radically change the course of your life for the better. You will feel more focused, motivated, and fulfilled.

Answer these questions to gain a clearer understanding of your life purpose.

- Have I been living my life purpose? If not, why?
- What advantages would I enjoy if I knew the purpose of my life?
- If I am hesitant to find my life purpose, why is that?
- Have I located at least three guided meditations on finding my life purpose?
- What is my end goal? How will things look when I live my purpose continuously?
- What can I do each day to move toward realizing my vision?
- How can I monetize my life purpose?
- What is my life purpose?

My prayer is that you will use this book as a tool to

transform your life. You too can live the life you deserve. This book is not meant to be read just once, it is meant to be a reference and a guide.

May God continue to transform, guide and direct you on your journey.

ACKNOWLEDGEMENTS

Writing a book is harder than I thought and more rewarding than I could have ever imagined. None of this would have been possible without the understanding and support of my husband, Roger Wright. He has given me grace and given me the space to spend countless hours writing and re-writing this book until it was finished. He is and will always be my biggest supporter. Thank you for all you do. I am eternally grateful. I appreciate all that you have done and continue to do. Thank you for all your help with this project, spending countless hours reviewing my manuscript. **I love you.**

I am eternally grateful to my mother who did all that she could to be the best mother and to love me with all her heart. Our start was not the best; however, you know the saying, "It's not how you start. It's how you finish." Mom, I am grateful for all the life lessons, bumpy roads, forgiveness, and love. I could not have written this story without the experiences we shared. I **love you.**

To my daughters Danielle, Destiny, and Rebekah, I am grateful God allowed me to be your mother and to love you. You all give me the courage to be the best version of myself, and you are the reason I have fought so hard to be better every day. Thank you for being my sideline cheerleaders. You inspire me. **I love you.**

Writing a book about your life is a surreal process. I am forever indebted to everyone that supported me. I could not have done this without you. A huge thank you to CaTyra Polland of Love for Words for the amazing developmental editing of my manuscript. Your work and customer service are phenomenal. Your understanding of my voice turned my manuscript into the book I wanted it to be. Thank you Erica James of MasterPieces Writing and Editing LLC for putting the icing on the cake with your amazing copy editing (proofreading) services.

Thank you Tyora Moody of Tywebbin Creations for your relentless patience with me as I sent my covers back to you what seemed like a million times. Thank you for giving me a phenomenal book cover. Thank you for bringing it to life. Oh, and let's not forget the formatting and social media packages—phenomenal.

Keep doing what you are doing; it truly changes lives. **Blessings to you.**

Thank you to the all-mighty King and Lord of my life, Jesus Christ. Without Him, I could not do anything. I am grateful for every single good and not-so-good experience in my life and the events that should have killed me or broken me. Instead, You saw fit to allow me to live and to share my story. I am forever grateful for everything and every day you have given me. Thank you, God, for never leaving my side and never changing your promise for my life. **I love you.**

About the Author

Shurvone Wright is a 5x published, best-selling author, motivational speaker, coach, the founder and CEO of Confidence Without Regret-The Butterfly Experience, and CEO of La' BossPreneur Marketing and Publishing LLC.She has been a guest on several radio shows including 97.5 FM Full Circle with Ms. Wanda to promote and discuss her journey and books. She is a contributing content writer for OWN IT digital magazine and Sistah's Place.

Shurvone's greatest passion is to help other women discover who they are and how to achieve all their dreams and goals. She helps women business owners and entrepreneurs with social media and business strategies to get a clear vision on how to attract their ideal client.

My Why !!

In Life you always have a reason why you work so hard and why you want to live you best life and walk in your purpose. My family means the world to me and I would do anything for them. I have worked hard to heal and live my best life, to walk in my purpose to leave a legacy for my children. Danielle, Destiny and Rebekah

Family is everything, I am so very blessed that God gave me our beautiful daughters, and amazing husband Roger. Let's not forget the beautiful granddaughter Naielle

Ptotographer-
DLightful Creation

The Wright Family

My Frist
Book Tour

119

Media
Exposure

Contact Shurvone Wright

SCHEDULE YOUR APPOINTMENT
- https://calendly.com/shurvone/social-media-strategy-call
- https://calendly.com/shurvone/schedulewithshurvone

SOCIAL MEDIA PLATFORMS
- https://www.instagram.com/la_bosspreneur_marketing
- https://www.instagram.com/author_shurvone
- https://www.linkedin.com/in/labosspreneur/
- https://www.facebook.com/shurvonepwright
- https://www.facebook.com group

WEBSITE
- https://www.Shurvonewright.com

EMAIL
- info@shurvonewright.com

NOTES

Made in the USA
Middletown, DE
24 October 2022

13405490R00086